THE TRENT
FAMILY
HISTORY

TRENT FAMILY GENEAOLOGY

Trent is an Anglo-Saxon name from the town of Trent in Dorset England. This town is along the Trent River. The Trent name was first found in Somerset, England where they had a family seat from ancient times. They have been there since before the Norman Conquest of 1066.

The Trent family was one of the earlier families to immigrate to the United States. They come from France and England and were settled here as early as 1673. Some of the maternal lines came to America as early as 1630. The other relatives are a mixture of races and cultures. These maternal family lines (the wives of the Trent men) came from Ireland, Germany, Switzerland and England.

There were huge Virginia landowners and friends with many of the original Virginia families. Some of them stayed in Virginia and this family line migrated to Hancock / Hawkins County, Tennessee around 1797.

The Trent family line is related to Thomas Jefferson, President of the United States. Please note the interesting relatives of Thomas Jefferson who are also related to the Branch line and Trent line. The Jefferson family connection is listed at the end of this book.

Please keep in mind that all the dates and facts aren't always 100% accurate due to census records, misspellings and sometimes incorrect (but close) dates of birth and death. Public records are not always accurate.

The importance of doing family history is so we can pass it along to our descendants. It is important and satisfying to know where and who we come from, the mixture of all our races and cultures. Knowing your family history gives you a sense of yourself. Many have great stories that can be passed down through the next generations.

SUMMARY OF THE GENERATIONS

GENERATION ONE: Phyllis Trent and Rodney Price

GENERATION TWO: Lincoln R. Trent (1905-1969) and Ida Mae Jackson (1905-1979) Hancock, County, TN

GENERATION THREE: Charles A. Trent (1879-1953) and Mattie Elizabeth Byrd (1882-1930) Both Hancock County, TN

GENERATION FOUR: William "Mack" Trent (1854-1874) and Martha Jane Wolfe (1855-1874) both Hancock County, TN

GENERATION FIVE: Zachariah Trent (1830-1880) and Susan Pratt (1837-1880) both from Hawkins County, TN

GENERATION SIX: Alexander Trent (1796-1893) and Mary Polly Martin (1797-1875) both born in Grayson, VA.

GENERATION SEVEN: William David Trent (1769-1866) and Charity Burton Osborne (1733-1820) both in Virginia territory.

GENERATION EIGHT: Alexander Trent III (1728-1793) and Elizabeth Frances Scott (1730-1780) both in Virginia.

GENERATION NINE: William Trent (1686-1768) and Ursula Branch (1693-1709) Henrico County, VA

GENERATION TEN: Henry Trent (1642-1701) and Elizabeth Sherman (1657-1732) both in Henrico County, VA

GENERATION ELEVEN: (Lord) Henry Trent Sr. (1624-1701) and Mary Alexander (1628-1641) Clara England to Virginia.

GENERATION TWELVE: Henri Trent (1591-1645) and Elizabeth Harris (1591-1632) Clara England to Virginia

THE FIRST FOUR GENERATIONS

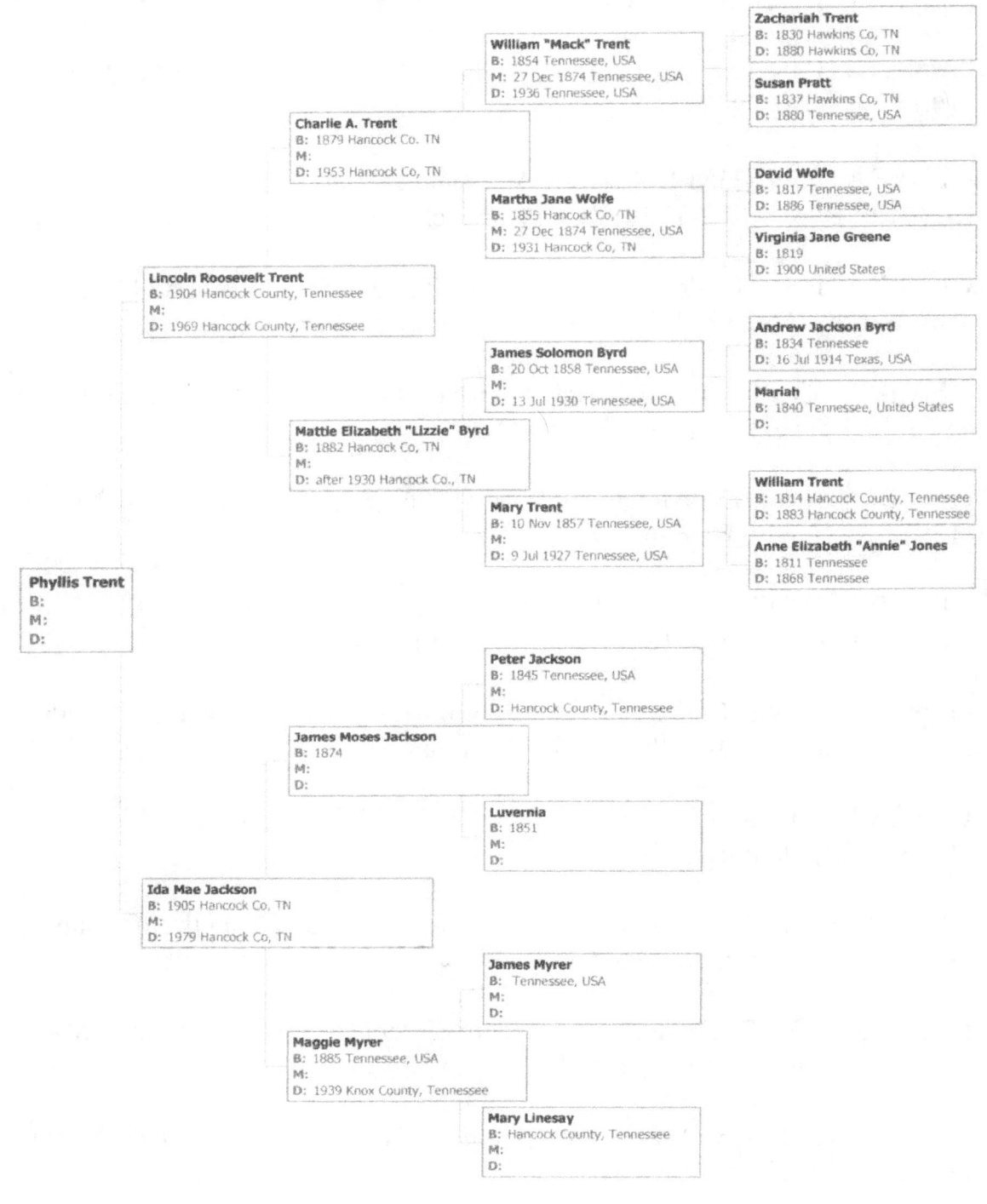

Zachariah Trent
B: 1830 Hawkins Co, TN
D: 1880 Hawkins Co, TN

Susan Pratt
B: 1837 Hawkins Co, TN
D: 1880 Tennessee, USA

William "Mack" Trent
B: 1854 Tennessee, USA
M: 27 Dec 1874 Tennessee, USA
D: 1936 Tennessee, USA

Charlie A. Trent
B: 1879 Hancock Co. TN
M:
D: 1953 Hancock Co, TN

David Wolfe
B: 1817 Tennessee, USA
D: 1886 Tennessee, USA

Virginia Jane Greene
B: 1819
D: 1900 United States

Martha Jane Wolfe
B: 1855 Hancock Co, TN
M: 27 Dec 1874 Tennessee, USA
D: 1931 Hancock Co, TN

Lincoln Roosevelt Trent
B: 1904 Hancock County, Tennessee
M:
D: 1969 Hancock County, Tennessee

Andrew Jackson Byrd
B: 1834 Tennessee
D: 16 Jul 1914 Texas, USA

Mariah
B: 1840 Tennessee, United States
D:

James Solomon Byrd
B: 20 Oct 1858 Tennessee, USA
M:
D: 13 Jul 1930 Tennessee, USA

Mattie Elizabeth "Lizzie" Byrd
B: 1882 Hancock Co, TN
M:
D: after 1930 Hancock Co., TN

William Trent
B: 1814 Hancock County, Tennessee
D: 1883 Hancock County, Tennessee

Anne Elizabeth "Annie" Jones
B: 1811 Tennessee
D: 1868 Tennessee

Mary Trent
B: 10 Nov 1857 Tennessee, USA
M:
D: 9 Jul 1927 Tennessee, USA

Phyllis Trent
B:
M:
D:

Peter Jackson
B: 1845 Tennessee, USA
M:
D: Hancock County, Tennessee

James Moses Jackson
B: 1874
M:
D:

Luvernia
B: 1851
M:
D:

Ida Mae Jackson
B: 1905 Hancock Co, TN
M:
D: 1979 Hancock Co, TN

James Myrer
B: Tennessee, USA
M:
D:

Maggie Myrer
B: 1885 Tennessee, USA
M:
D: 1939 Knox County, Tennessee

Mary Linesay
B: Hancock County, Tennessee
M:
D:

4

GENERATIONS FIVE TO EIGHT:

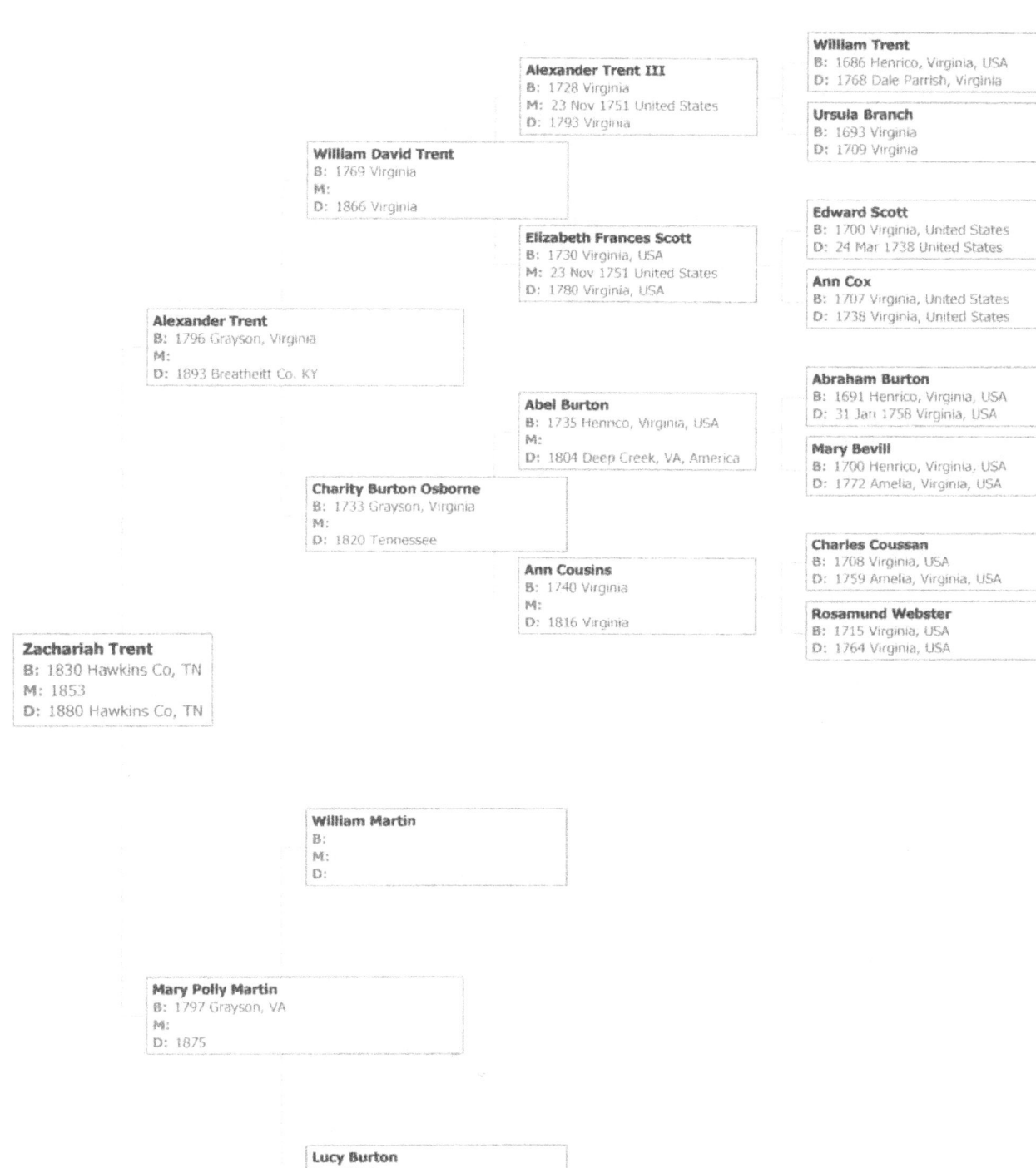

William Trent
B: 1686 Henrico, Virginia, USA
D: 1768 Dale Parrish, Virginia

Ursula Branch
B: 1693 Virginia
D: 1709 Virginia

Alexander Trent III
B: 1728 Virginia
M: 23 Nov 1751 United States
D: 1793 Virginia

Edward Scott
B: 1700 Virginia, United States
D: 24 Mar 1738 United States

Ann Cox
B: 1707 Virginia, United States
D: 1738 Virginia, United States

William David Trent
B: 1769 Virginia
M:
D: 1866 Virginia

Elizabeth Frances Scott
B: 1730 Virginia, USA
M: 23 Nov 1751 United States
D: 1780 Virginia, USA

Alexander Trent
B: 1796 Grayson, Virginia
M:
D: 1893 Breatheitt Co. KY

Abraham Burton
B: 1691 Henrico, Virginia, USA
D: 31 Jan 1758 Virginia, USA

Mary Bevill
B: 1700 Henrico, Virginia, USA
D: 1772 Amelia, Virginia, USA

Abel Burton
B: 1735 Henrico, Virginia, USA
M:
D: 1804 Deep Creek, VA, America

Charity Burton Osborne
B: 1733 Grayson, Virginia
M:
D: 1820 Tennessee

Charles Coussan
B: 1708 Virginia, USA
D: 1759 Amelia, Virginia, USA

Rosamund Webster
B: 1715 Virginia, USA
D: 1764 Virginia, USA

Ann Cousins
B: 1740 Virginia
M:
D: 1816 Virginia

Zachariah Trent
B: 1830 Hawkins Co, TN
M: 1853
D: 1880 Hawkins Co, TN

William Martin
B:
M:
D:

Mary Polly Martin
B: 1797 Grayson, VA
M:
D: 1875

Lucy Burton
B: 1789 Tennessee
M:
D: After 1850

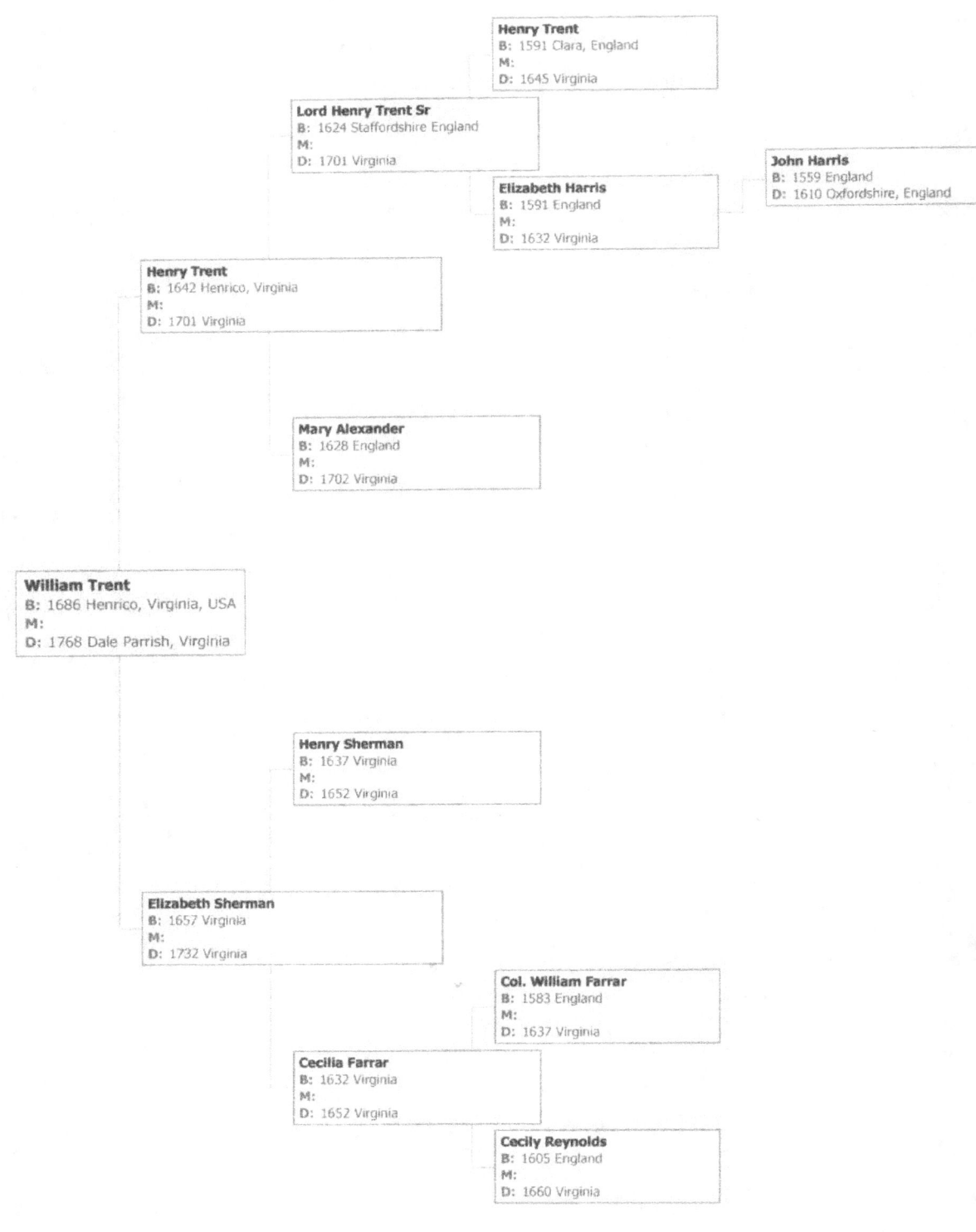

Henry Trent
B: 1591 Clara, England
M:
D: 1645 Virginia

Lord Henry Trent Sr
B: 1624 Staffordshire England
M:
D: 1701 Virginia

John Harris
B: 1559 England
D: 1610 Oxfordshire, England

Elizabeth Harris
B: 1591 England
M:
D: 1632 Virginia

Henry Trent
B: 1642 Henrico, Virginia
M:
D: 1701 Virginia

Mary Alexander
B: 1628 England
M:
D: 1702 Virginia

William Trent
B: 1686 Henrico, Virginia, USA
M:
D: 1768 Dale Parrish, Virginia

Henry Sherman
B: 1637 Virginia
M:
D: 1652 Virginia

Elizabeth Sherman
B: 1657 Virginia
M:
D: 1732 Virginia

Col. William Farrar
B: 1583 England
M:
D: 1637 Virginia

Cecilia Farrar
B: 1632 Virginia
M:
D: 1652 Virginia

Cecily Reynolds
B: 1605 England
M:
D: 1660 Virginia

These are the generations each in detail:

GENERATION ONE:
Phyllis Trent & Rodney Price

GENERATION TWO:

Lincoln Roosevelt Trent (1905-1969) and Ida Mae Jackson (1905-1979)
    Buried at Byrd / Trent cemetery

Ida Mae Jackson

Ida's parents were James Moses Jackson and Maggie Myrer.
Ida's mother Maggie Myrer Jackson was born in Grainger County, TN in 1885. She died at the hospital in Knox County, TN in 1939. She had cancer of the pancreas. Ida's grandparents are Peter Jackson (1845) and Luvernia (1851) on the Jackson side and James Myrer and Mary Linesay.

Their children: Still living so I won't put them in public record.

GENERATION THREE:

Charlie A. Trent (1879-1953) and Mattie Elizabeth Byrd (1882-1930)
Charlie was a school teacher, well known merchant and holder of different County offices.

Mattie's parents were Solomon Byrd (1858-1930)and Mary Trent (1857-1927). Mattie's grandparents are William Trent (1814-1883) and mother Anne Elizabeth "Annie" Jones (1811-1866). William's father was William D. Trent and Charity Burton Osborne found in the section below.

Mary Trent (Mattie's mother) was married first to Lee Greene, 2nd to Joab Alexander Brewer and last to James Solomon "Sol" Byrd. She was the grandmother of the country music star, Buck Trent, through her first daughter Alice Greene who married Kimbrow Trent and Buck Trent was their son. She had eight children by Sol Byrd but only 4 of them lived.

The Byrd/Trent cemetery in Hancock County, Tennessee is where most of them are buried.

Their children:

Ollie May married Chester Mahan (1903-1972)
Lincoln R. married Ida Mae Jackson
Alice,
Alonzo,
Myrtle,
Donald,
Bonnie

Charlie A. Trent and wife Mattie Elizabeth "Lizzie" Byrd

Charlie A. Trent and wife Mattie Elizabeth Byrd

Charlie Alfred Trent and Mattie Elizabeth Byrd

Charlie Alfred Trent and wife, Mattie Elizabeth Byrd

Description of photo and the boys:
Description: L to R Grant Mahan, James Miner, Kyle Lawson, Lon Winstead, Arley Stapleton, **Lincoln Trent, ? C.A.[Charlie] Trent**, David Winkles.

GENERATION FOUR:

William "Mack" Trent (1854-1936) and Martha J. Wolfe (1855-1931) Martha's parents were David Wolfe (1817-1886) and Virginia Jane Greene (1819-1900). The Wolfe family line came from Germany. See the story below.

Martha Wolfe's parents were David Wolfe (1817-1886) born in Grainger, TN and died in Hancock Co, Tn and Virginia Jane Greene (1819-1900). Her grandparents were Adam Wolfe (1784-1862) born in NC and died in Grainger, TN and Jemima McCoy (1792-1873).

Marth'a great grandparents were John Wolfe (1751-1811) and Catherine Bare (1753-1835). John Wolfe was born in York, Pennslyvania and he died in Copper Creek, Russell Virginia. Catherine Bare was from Lee, Virginia. Martha's great great grandparents were from Germany and settled in Pennsylvania. This line goes on to John Nicholas Wolfe (1725-1810) and Anna Maria Bressler (1726-1824). Further generations go back to a place called <u>Steinsfurt, Rhein-Neckar-Kreis, Baden-Wuerttemberg, Germany</u>. The line goes back to 1521 Zurich, Switzerland.

Their children: *many are in the photo below

Silas (1876-1935) married Rachell Drinnon
Joe Abb (1878) married Valina Osborne
Charlie A., married Mattie Elizabeth "Lizzie" Byrd
Audie married Mary Brown and also married Mary Russell Lincoln married
Lavana Roberts
Ervin married Ethel Stableton
Harrison,
Ida Mae married James Winstead
Frank W. (1875) married Mendie Greene
Milium
Roy married Nellie Gilbert

Description of picture:
Description: Small girl on left is Cordie, daughter of Audie Trent. Back row, left to right: Silas Trent, Roy Trent, Charlie Trent (all children of Martha and Mack Trent). Man sitting down in front row is William Mack Trent (b. Dec 33, 1854; d. June 1931) and his wife, Martha Wolfe Lawson (b. June 17, 1854, d. 1931). Boy between them is their grandson, Roy Trent's son. Girl on right is Mae Trent, daughter of William and Martha. William Mack is the son of Zachariah and Susan Pratt. Martha is the daughter of Elder David and Virginia Jane Greene Wolfe.

Description of second family picture is Back row, left to right: Irving, Audi, Silas, and Charlie Trent Grown man sitting is William Mack Trent and his wife, Martha J Wolfe. Boys at the bottom on left is Coy Trent, William Mack is holding Roy; little girl at the bottom right is Mae. This photo was provided by Ms. Kay Lawson Jarvis

THE STORY OF JOHN WOLFE – Martha's great grandfather

- John Wolfe was born about December 27, 1751 and lived about 25 miles north of Winchester in Berkeley County, (West) Virginia, at the time of his marriage about 1778 to Catherine Bare. He was known as a "genteel, sober young man," although neither he nor his wife was educated; neither could read or write. About four months after the marriage, he was present when a murder was committed; the murderer was hanged, and although Wolfe was only a witness, he fled in 1778 to South Carolina and Georgia for over a year; he then returned and immediately took his wife and child to North Carolina.

  In the spring of 1788, the family moved to a farm on the south side of the North Fork of the Holston River; they were extremely poor, but on December 6, 1790, he bought 50 acres where he then lived from John Kearns, and on November 14, 1796, 150 acres from Dennis Coudry. The land located at the junction of the river with the Tennessee state line about four miles from Gate City.

  John Wolfe was a strict, hard-working, and careful farmer and he accumulated a sizeable estate worth about $3,000.00 by 1806. He also peddled whiskey in the Clinch River settlements and may have traded horses in Kentucky. He also leased land to Robert Stubblefield. In 1792 his brother-in-law, Peter Bare, lived with him for about four months.

  After several years, Wolfe's mental condition began to deteriorate as he became increasingly depressed about his part in the murder he had witnessed many years before. He sometimes realized when his fits of depression were coming on and would warn his family to stay away from him. However, according to Joseph Duncan, an employee, "sometimes he would immediately go to drinking and quarreling with his family and at other times he would pass over the course of a night before he would break out so very bad, during which times he and his wife would generally talk Dutch together...and he would make all fly." He threatened his family with physical violence and made many extravagant and scandalous statements about them.

His condition became worse after about 1803, when a blackmailer named Stunn came to Wolfe, falsely claiming he had killed Stunn's father; he also claimed to have a warrant for Wolfe's arrest but stated he would accept a horse as the price for not prosecuting. Stunn was arrested, but escaped, and after this incident, Wolfe lost interest in his family and property as he became more depressed. Life in the home became increasingly difficult, so that Caty Wolfe sent her daughter Hannah to live with her aunt Mary Pope in June, 1805, and her son Adam to live with his uncle Charles Wolfe in Tennessee. Wolfe threatened to desert his family, and after severe emotional attack, he sold his 200 acre farm to John Weaver on February. 13, 1806, for considerably less that it was worth. He then took his youngest son, Jacob, and went to the Moravian settlement near Winston-Salem, North Carolina, where he apprenticed the boy to a saddler and loaned his money out at interest.

On April 12, 1806, after Wolfe had gone to North Carolina, his sons Henry and John forced John Weaver to return to them the 200 acre farm; Henry got a patent to the land in 1809. Then on September 15, 1806, they agreed to furnish their mother the house where she lived, and each year to provide her with a half acre of flax land, 50 bushels of Indian corn, 400 pounds of pork, a bushel of salt, eight bushels of wheat, hay or fodder, a half acre of cotton land, fruit, pasture, firewood, three pairs of shoes, and $4.00 cash.

About a year later, John Wolfe returned to his family on the Holston and stayed with them about a year. He then lived in the home of Jacob Peters for about two years and then bought 250 acres on Copper Creek in Russell County, Virginia. He hanged himself there in January, 1811 and his personal debts were settled and his estate sold in 1816.

The Wolfe family was involved in several lawsuits concerning the pro-perty, as Caty and her younger children sought a share in the land that Henry and John Wolfe had acquired from Weaver; it was eventually divided in 1821 among all the heirs. Henry Wolfe sold his mother 137 acres of the farm on January 25, 1814, for $500.00; she sold the land on June 27, 1828; to her son-in-law, Abraham Lane, with whom she subsequently made her home until her death about 1835 in Scott County, Virginia.

GENERATION FIVE:

Zachariah Trent (1830-1880) Hawkins County, TN and Susan Pratt (1837-1880). Zachariah was a farmer.

Susan Pratt's parents were James Stephen Pratt (1800-1849) and Polly Osborne. Her grandparents were Thomas Pratt (1759-1838) and Sarah Garrison (1759-1852). Her Great grandparents were John Pratt (1718-1785) and Rebecca Sarah Vernon (1728-1809) from Virginia. The Pratt family line goes back to 1359 Suffolk, England.

Their children were:

William "Mack", 1854-1936 married Martha Jane Wolfe
Mary Polly 1871-
George, 1859 married Lula Buttry
Royal 1860-
Lucy – 1864
May – 1858
Richard 1867
James, 1869
Freelin 1865 married Carolyn Miner
Hasque, 1878 married Cordie Rider
Sarah, 1875

GENERATION SIX

Alexander Trent (1796-1893) and Mary Polly Martin (1797-1875)

Alexander was born in Grayson, VA and lived in Hawkins County, TN and died in Breathitt, KY

Mary Polly Martin's parents were William Martin and Lucy Burton.

Children with Mary Polly Martin

John
William 1817-1858 married Mary Polly Baker
Richard 1819-1883

David 1820-1859
Thomas 1822-1870 married Sarah _____
Elizabeth Betty – 1826-1886
Ann Graves – 1827-1913
Isiah – 1828
Zachariah – 1828-1880 married Susan Pratt
Lucinda Lucy – 1830-1873
Pleasant M. 1831-1860 married Albira Berry (1834-1907) He died in the
Civil War
Jesse 1836-1910
James Madison 1841-1902 married Zana Brewer Seals (1843-1936)

GENERATION SEVEN

William D. Trent (1770-1866) and Charity Burton Osborne (1773-1820)
They were both from Grayson, VA.   Charity Burton's parents were Abel
Burton and Ann Cousins. He also married Margaret Peggy Martin.

William D. Trent was the wealthiest man in the county with
real estate estimated near $50,000 in 1883 when he died. He died
of a stomach ulcer. He migrated from Virginia to Trent Valley, Hancock TN
in 1798.

Their children:

Known children of William D. Trent, Sr. and Charity Burton Osborne are:

- Stepson: James Burton (Osborne?) Trent, born about 1795, died after 1860. This child was actually William D. Trent's stepson, but in later years he used the Trent name, although he fought in the War of 1812 under the name James Burton. James was born in Grayson County, Virginia in 1795. He married Elizabeth Johnson, born in 1799 in North Carolina. She died in the 1900's. Stories are that she lived in three centuries. They were farmers in Hancock County, Tennessee.

  James Trent's descendants are known as "Snowbirds". They don't know if it was James or one of his sons...Henry Cloud was told it was one of his sons, Rev. William Trent. (both were short men and it could have been either) The story goes he was a small man and so very active, he could move and jump about so quickly that you could hardly keep up with him. One day a group of men were chatting or gossiping and it was supposed that he got pretty carried away, so a member of the group of men said, "Hey, James, (or William whichever it was) you remind me of a snowbird." From that day on it has stuck...They do the same thing to differentiate the Lawsons (wheat breads, coons, etc.) There are also "Sop" Trents...The needed a way to identify just which Bill, Dave, Jim, or Jesse they were speaking of.

Alexander Trent, born 18 Dec 1796, died 4 Nov 1873, married Mary "Polly" Martin. Obituary: Brother Alexander Trent, the subject of this notice, was born in Hancock County, Tennessee about the 18th of December, 1797. He professed faith in Christ and was baptized into the fellowship of the Baptist Church when he was about 36 years old. He was shortly afterwards ordained to the office of Deacon which position he maintained with credit, and made himself useful to the church.

As a husband and father, he was kind and affectionate, generous to the poor, and liberal in his contributions for the support of the churches. His house was the preacher's home. A great many ministers preached in his house and members of souls were happily converted to God under his roof. He died at his residence in Hancock County, Tennessee on the 4th of November, 1873. His health had been declining for some time though he was confined to his house but a few days previous to his death. He bore his afflictions with great patience and Christian resignation, often speaking to his brethren in glowing terms of his confidence in Christ, and his hopes of companionship with beatified spirits in his Heavenly Father's kingdom. His sun went down without a cloud, to rise in eternal splendor, and his body was quietly laid away in the great charnel house of the dead, there to sleep till the voice of the Son of God shall summon him forth in immortal youth and vigor. He leaves a wife and a large offspring to mourn his loss.

Virginia Jane "Jensie" Trent, born about 1800, died after 1870, married Richard Greene.

Zachariah G. Trent, born about 1801, died after 1850/1860, married Naomi Greene, and later Matilda Hoffman (or Coffman).

Mary "Polly" Trent, born 8 Feb 1803. She married (1) Timothy Holdaway about 1823. He died about 1835 in St. Clair Co., Illinois. Mary married (2) William Lunceford, 5 Nov 1837, in St. Clair Co., Ill. William died 16 Oct 1876 in San Luis Obispo, Ca, at the age of 80. There were 4 children.
.

Elizabeth "Betty" Trent, born about 1807 in then, Hawkins Co., TN. She married Jesse Cope, 1 Aug 1820 in Hawkins Co., TN. He was born 4 Oct 1802. Jesse died 24 Mar 1873, at the age of 70. Elizabeth died after 22 Mar 1891 in Hancock, Co., TN. She also married Thomas Martin.

Mahala "Haley" Trent, born about 1808 in then, Hawkins Co., TN. She married Thomas Martin about 1831 in then, Hawkins Co., TN; they divorced. Thomas died in Hancock Co., TN. Mahala died after 22 Mar 1891 probably in Hancock Co., TN. Her children were Christopher, William, Mary, Charity and Margaret Martin.
.

Richard Trent, born about 1810, died after 1860, married Elizabeth Jones. She was a sister to Wm. D. Trent, Jr.'s wife, Annie Jones.

William D. "Billy" Trent, Jr., born 17 Jun 1814, died 28 Jun 1883. He married Annie Jones. These are the parents of Martha Mae Trent, who married Jesse Burton Greene, and James Austin Trent who married Mary Jane Greene.
.

David Trent, born about 1820, died Feb 1859. He married Manerva Hawk. He also married Margaret Peggy Martin.

Editor (Hallie Garner)'s note: There could have been other children, as there are some lengthy time periods between children. Certainly, there were no other children involved in his estate settlement.

GREAT STORY ABOUT WILLIAM D. TRENT AND FAMILY:
http://www.angelfire.com/tv/trent/wdtrent.html

From "Cantwell-Greene Families of East Tennessee"
Book by Hallie Price Garner

William D. Trent, Sr. was the father of Zachariah G. Trent and at least 9 other children. He was the son of Alexander Trent and an Elizabeth Frances Scott. His mother may have been an Indian but no documentation has been found. He was born about 1770 in Virginia and died about 1866. "There have been many stories of Indian blood in the Wm. D. Trent line. These stories are enhanced by the unusual symbol on one of the burial sheds in the James A. Trent Cemetery......."

"Researcher Earl Cole states that the original research on the Trent family was done by the late Alton Lee Greene of Sanger, Texas. We know from Alton's genealogical records that he interviewed many older residents and learned the old stories. Alton related to Earl that the Indian ancestor was not from the Charity Burton line, but through William D. Trent Sr.'s so that would have meant Wm. D. Jr's mother's line, but again, we unfortunately have no proof."...quoted from Hallie Garner's book.

William D. Trent, Sr. and Henry Trent are believed to be full brothers and half-brother to Alexander Trent's other children, one of whom was Alexander. **He and his half-brother William, are by legend, the first settlers of Trent Valley, Hancock Co., TN.** He and his brother are supposed to have married Burton sisters on the same day in Grayson Co., VA with the marriage ceremony performed by the Baptist minister Vincent Jones (May 19, 1843 Hawkins Co., TN revolutionary war pension application for Jane Burton Trent). Alexander applied for a pension in June 1834 which was witnessed by his neighbor Enoch Osborne. In it, he says he joined in 1777 from Bedford Co.

William, Sr. married Charity Burton Osborne. Charity and Alexander's wife, Jane Burton, were said to be sisters. Charity was born about 1773-1776 in Virginia. We believe Charity died in about March 1847, because William, Sr. was married to Margaret "Peggy" (Martin) Winstead (a widow) by the time of the 1850 census. Charity Burton was most likely a descendant of John Burton, the immigrant who patented his plantation "Longfield" in 1665. Records indicate that some of his descendents lived in Chesterfield, Bedford, and Campbell Counties, and marriages often took place within families that knew each other.

MIGRATION TO TENNESSEE
"William D. Trent, Sr. was born 1770 in Virginia, no record of his death. He met and married Jane's sister, Charity Burton Osborne, born in Virginia in

1773 and died in the 1820's. She was a widow, with a child named James Osborne. James later changed his name to Trent, and went through life as a Trent.

In 1798, an Uncle William Williamson Trent, his wife, Sarah Susanna____, along with his unmarried daughter, Nancy and his son, William Williamson Trent, Jr. and his wife Nancy Potts Trent; her sister, Hannah Potts Lawson and her husband, Drury Lawson; our **William and Charity Burton Trent**; and Alexander and Jane Burton Trent and their children all leave Chesterfield County, VA. and move around in the Southwestern counties of VA Finally they arrive in what is now called Hancock County, TN."
Note: Taken from Alton Greene's (Green Family book).

OBITUARY: obituary, published in Distant Crossroads quoting from the Morristown Gazette, 4 Jul 1883.
....DATELINE SNEEDVILLE Wm. D. Trent, an old and respected citizen of his county, died on Saturday, the 23d, int. and buried on Sunday, a large number of friends and relatives attending the funeral services. Mr. Trent, without an exception, was the wealthiest citizen of our county. His property, all nearly consisted of real estate, worth something near $50,000.

And again in the Morristown Gazette August 1, 1883:
....On the 23rd of June 1883 at his home near Sneedville, Hancock Co., TN, at 9 o'clock a.m. William D. Trent died in about the 70th year of his age, of something like ulceration of his stomach, and was buried on Sunday morning the 25th, at his home in the presence of a large concourse of persons, who followed him to his last resting place, where the funeral rites were performed by Rev. Lloyd Davis. He was born and raised near where he died. LMJ.

(Editor (Hallie Garnar)'s note: I suspect these initials were for Louis M. Jarvis who was administrator of his William Sr.'s estate.)

GENERATION EIGHT:

Alexander Trent Sr. (1728-1793) born Henrico, VA and died Patrick, VA. He died being scalped by Indians in Patrick County, VA. He married Elizabeth Scott from Manikin Goochland, VA (1730-1780). She was a Cherokee Indian we think. He reportedly married three times.

Their Children were:

Alexander Trent Jr. 1759-1841 married Jane Burton /fought in the Revolutionary War. Jane is the sister of Charity Burton Osborne.
William D. Trent Sr. 1769-1866 married Charity Burton Osborne
Lumina "Mina" 1752-1838
Henry 1753-1834
Elijah 1755-1814
Zachariah – 1758-1822
Benjamin 1760
Frances 1762-1845
Field 1766-1799

Before you read the following information keep in mind that Alexander's father died and gave two of his brother's Indian woman in his will:

"From this deed, we learn the name of Alexander's wife, Elizabeth, but we do not know who she was, or if she was the only wife. Family stories handed down in several branches of the family suggest several scenarios:
----- 1)that he married an Indian woman and that her name was Elizabeth,
----- 2)he had two wives, and the second one was named Elizabeth,
-----or 3)he was married first to Alexander Trent, Jr's mother, second to an Indian woman who was William D.'s mother, and third to a woman named Elizabeth who signed the 1792 deed. Very little is actually known about Alexander Trent's wives, so this is conjecture only.

These conjectures are made because old Hancock County stories always said that Alexander Trent, Jr, The Revolutionary War Soldier (RWS), and William D. Trent were half brothers and that William D. Trent's mother was Indian (see some later quotations I will include)."

"Other children of Alexander (third generation) are: Alexander (RWS), (married Jane Burton), Zachariah, Henry, Mima, Elijah, Benjamin, Francis, and Field Trent. We do not know if any of these were full siblings to William or if they were half, but we do know that Alexander (RWS) was always said to be William D.'s half brother."

Other info from Hallie: "In Alexander Trent, Jr's Revolutionary War Pension application R10695, (made many years later when he lived in Hawkins

County, Tennessee) he stated that he was born in Chesterfield County, Virginia in 1759 and that he lived in Bedford County, Virginia when he enlisted in the American Revolution in 1777."

GENERATION NINE

William Trent (1686-1768) and Ursula Branch (1693-1768)
William was born in Henrico, VA and died in Chesterfield, VA. Ursula was also from Henrico, VA.

Their children:
William 1715-1797
 Alexander William III 1728-1793 married Elizabeth Scott (perhaps an Indian) and was scalped by Indians in Patrick County, VA.
 Benjamin 1717-1797
Henry 1734-1808
Lucy 1712-1799 married a Perrin Giles

WILL OF WILLIAM TRENT:
from Maxine Vernon:
Will of William Trent of Dale Parish, Chesterfield Co., VA, Will book 2, page 204
To my son Alexander - 1 negro Sarah and items
To son William 1 Indian woman named Judith and horse
To son Benjamin all my hogs
To son Henry - 1 Indian woman named Moll and chest
To daughter Lucy Giles - my share of crop and feather bed
To my housekeeper Elizabeth Baley - livestock
Executor: Son Alexander
Witnesses: Antony Taylor, James Taylor, Nathaniel Lacy

* William Trent's aunt, Ann Sherman, married Ursula's uncle, Christopher Branch.

* William Trent's brother, Henry, married Edith Harris, Ursula's 1st cousin 1x removed.

* Another brother, Alexander, married Obedience Branch, Ursula's 1st cousin.

Ursula Branch was under 21 when her father died in 1700. Based on court records, Marsh estimates Ursula would have been 17 or 18 in 1709, the year William and Ursula Trent were probably married.

GENERATION TEN

Henry Trent (1649-1701) Henrico Co, VA
and Elizabeth Sherman (1657-1732) all in Varina parish Henrico, VA

Elizabeth's parents are Henry Sherman and Cecilia Farrar. Cecilia's parents were Col. William Farrar (1583 England to 1637 Virginia) and Cecily Reynolds (1605 England to 1660 Virginia).

Elizabeth's mother, **Cecilia Reynolds family goes back to 1404 Nottinghamshire and Devon England**.

Cecilia Farrar's grandparents were John Farrar and Cecily Kelke from England. John's father William Farrar married Margaret Lacy. **The Lacy family goes back to 1355 Yorkshire England.**

The Lacy family is also connected to Richard Archdeacon, born 1304 in Cornwall England. He died in 1371 in Tintagel Castle. **This Lacy line goes even farther back to Odo Archdeacon and beyond dated 1047 Yorkshire, England.**

Their children:
Alexander 1674-1703 married Obedience Branch (Ursula's first cousin) and daughter of John and Martha branch.

Henry – 1676-1726 married a cousin of Thomas Jefferson, Edith Harris (Ursula's cousin once removed) Edith Harris is the daughter of Thomas Harris and Mary Jefferson. After Henry's death Edith married John Osborne and later Peter Patrick. Mary Jefferson is a direct ancestor of Thomas

Jefferson. ** See the President Thomas Jefferson connection through the Branch family.

William – 1686-1768 lived in Chesterfield VA. Married Ursula Branch
John 1678-1760 married Elizabeth ____
Susanna 1686-1730 married William Womack and Daniel Nunnary
Mary 1682-1734 married Richard Cox
Rebecca 1684-1731 married ____ Wacher

TRENTS ON THE "Ten Thousand Name" Petition

The Ten Thousand Name petition was presented during the first Virginia General Assembly session on October 16, 1776 asking for disestablishment of the church of England as wells as religions equality, this document consisted of 125 pages sewn or joined together with wax seals and was signed by an unprecedented ten thousand Virginia Citizens. Henry Trent Sr. Henry Trent, William Trent, and Benjamin Trent names are included in the list

The earliest mention of Henry Trent in Virginia records is 1673, when he claimed headrights to 200 acres on the James River in Henrico County for bringing himself and three other people to Virginia.

The London Company granted "headrights" to encourage immigration to Virginia. If a person paid for his voyage to Virginia, he received 50 acres of land. If he paid for others as well, he got 50 acres for each of them.

It would be wrong to conclude that Henry Trent arrived in America shortly before obtaining the grant in 1673. Often headrights were claimed long after the immigrants came to Virginia. And if a person traveled to England, then returned to Virginia, they could claim headrights to their second voyage as well. Transport to Virginia from another colony qualified as well.

On Nov. 7, 1673, the day Henry Trent receives his 200, his future father-in-law, Henry Sherman, receives 228 acres in Henrico County, though on the south side of the James River.

Henry and Elizabeth Sherman had four sons and two daughters. The oldest son, Alexander, though he died young and left only one son, founded a line of wealthy landowners who married into some of Colonial Virginia's most prominent families. Alexander's grandson, Alexander of Cumberland County, served in the Colonial legislature before the American Revolution. Alexander and his brother, Peterfield, were prosperous merchants.

Henry and Elizabeth's second son, Henry, also prospered, marrying a cousin of Thomas Jefferson. This Henry had one son, also named Henry, who lived in Goochland County and apparently moved to Grannel County, N.C., before his death.

Little has been found about John Trent or his descendants. The fourth son, William, lived in the Swift Creek area of Chesterfield County. He married Ursula, who may have been a Branch, but this hasn't been proven. After William's death, at least two of his sons, Alexander and Henry, moved to Campbell County, while another, William, moved to Henry County, Va.

Most of the Trent's in early Virginia appear to have descended from Henry and Elizabeth, but many questions remain. Prominent among the mysteries are the identities of the Henry Trent who amassed hundreds of acres in Albemarle and left a will in Amherst County in 1796 and the Thomas Trent who was wounded in the Revolutionary War and settled in Buckingham County.

NOTE: This account is heavily indebted to the research of Barbara R. Marsh and Ron Walters.

Events------------------------------
Nov. 7, 1673: Henry Trent receives 200 acres in Henrico County on the north side of the James River for transporting to Virginia four people, Charles Tyre, Henry Trent, Margaret Rayes and Alice Sleek. On the same day, his future father-in-law, Henry Sherman, received 228 acres in Henrico County, though on the south side of the James River.

April 1, 1701: Will of Henry Trent recorded (written Jan. 8, 1700). He leaves each of his sons, Alexander, Henry, John and William, 109 acres in Varina Parish. William gets first choice when the land is divided. Henry gets a cow at Richard Cox's. His daughter, Mary Cox, wife of Richard Cox, receives a gold ring; daughters Rebecca Trent and Susanna Trent receive 2,000 pounds of tobacco each. His widow, Elizabeth gets three servants.

GENERATION ELEVEN:

Henry Sr. Trent (1624-1701) and Mary Alexander (1628-1702)
He was born in Clara, Staffordshire, England
He immigrated to this country in 1673. He ended up in Henrico, VA
He died in Henderson County, Rusk Texas. She was born in Staffordshire
England and immigrated to Henrico, VA.

Their children:
James, 1646-1701
William, 1651-1724
Henry Jr., 1642-1701
Alexander 1658-1703
Rebecca 1654-1735

GENERATION TWELVE:

Henri Trent (1591-1645) and Elizabeth Harris (1590-1632) born in Clara,
Staffordshire, England, died in Henrico, VA.   Elizabeth Harris's father was
John Harris. It is said that Henri Trent is the son of French immigrants. The
spelling of his name also is French.

Children:

William Junior, 1625-1701
Maurice, 1627-1700
Henry Sr. 1624-1701
James

THE THOMAS JEFFERSON CONNECTION

Ursula Branch married William Trent (see above) Ursula Branch's father was Samuel Branch (1663-1700) and Ursula Goode
Her grandparents were Christopher Branch (1628 VA-1665) and Sarah Almond (1629 Henrico, VA to 1666 Virginia). Her mother Sarah remarried to a Walter Scott in 1707. It was Ursula's Aunt, Mary who married Thomas Jefferson, and they became the great grandparents of President Thomas Jefferson.

Ursula's grandfather Christopher Branch was the great great grandfather of Thomas Jefferson. Her great grandparents were Christopher Branch (1601-) and Mary Addie.

It is the Branch family that is related to Thomas Jefferson.

This is the information on Christopher Branch (1601)
> So Christopher Branch came on the ship the ***London Merchant*** in 1620, and was at "College Land" after the massacre of 1622. Christopher had a son Thomas only 9 months old at that time.
>
> Christopher came to Virginia in the ship London Merchant in March, 1619-1620, and settled in the present Henrico County where they were living "att yeColledg Land" in February 1623-4 with their son Thomas 2 Branch, nine months old. Christopher" Branch later patented land and first lived at or near Arrowhattocks on the north side of James River finally settling at Kingsland on the south side of the river (almost opposite Arrowhattocks) in the present Chesterfield County, near Proctor's Creek, at that time, and for many years afterwards, Henrico. Christopher' Branch was one of the viewers of tobacco in Henrico in 1639 and in an Assembly convened January 1639 was one of the representatives for Henrico County in the House of Burgesses, Henrico County, Virginia and was in 1656 Justice of the Peace, Henrico County, Virginia
>
> **OTHER INFORMATION ON CHRISTOPHER BRANCH:**
> Christopher Branch was the son of Lionel Branch of London, Gentleman, grandson of William Branch of Abingdon, Berkshire, Gentleman, and great grandson of Richard Branch of Abingdon,

Woolendraper. Christopher Branch is himself styled "gentleman" in the record of his marriage.

The Branch lines goes back to 1509 with Richard Branch from Berkshire England. The Christopher Branch (1601) is also a descendant of Lady Godiva (1010-1086) and King Henry I (1068-1135).

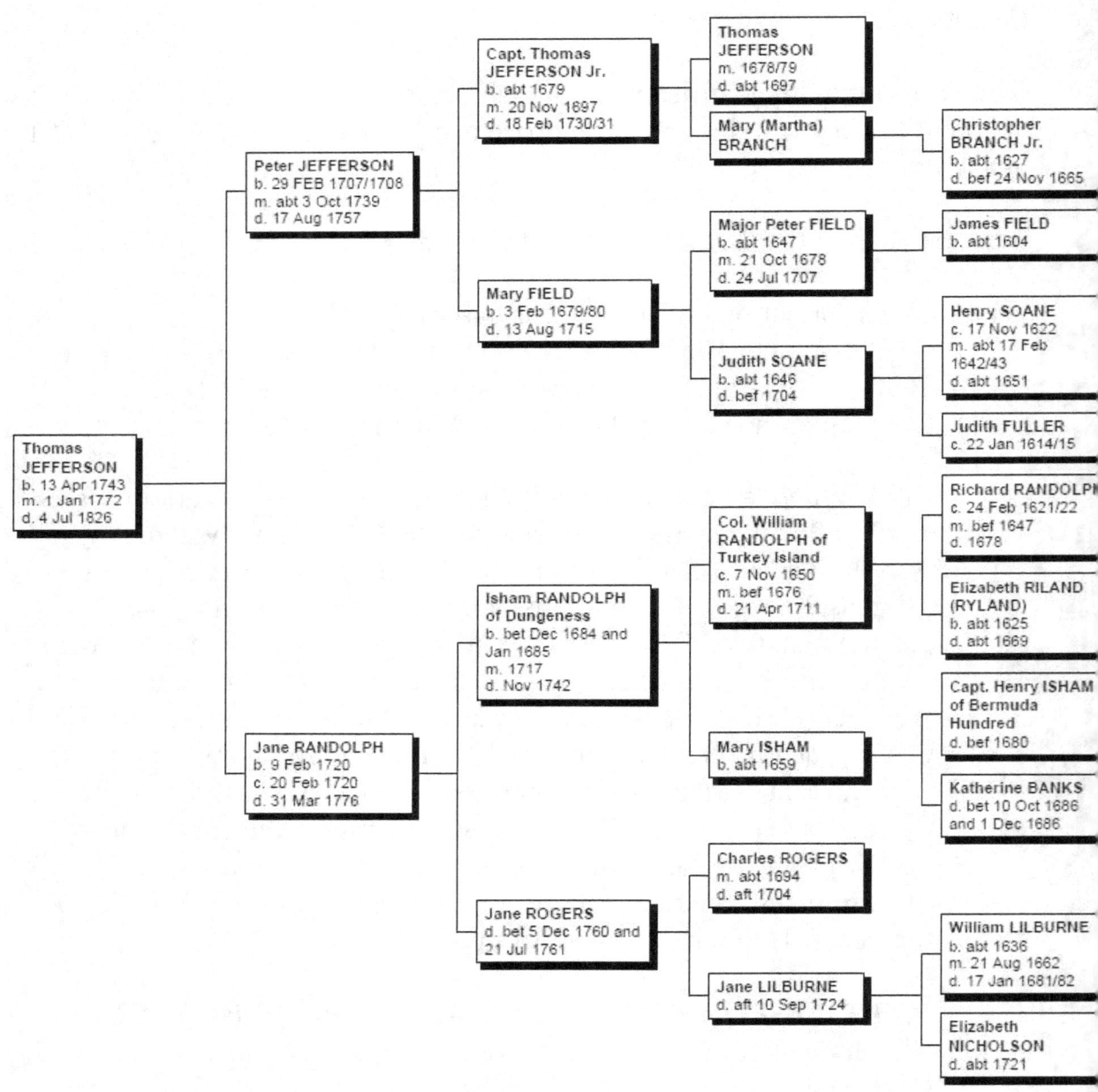

THE RELATIVES OF PRESIDENT THOMAS JEFFERSON / and The
Branch / Trent families. This is a very impressive list.

There may be many relationships between President Jefferson and each of the following Famous Kin. Only the ancestors for some of the closest relationships are displayed for each person listed below.

President **Thomas JEFFERSON** was born 13 April 1743 in Shadwell,
Virginia, to **Peter JEFFERSON** and **Jane RANDOLPH**. His father Peter
Jefferson was a wealthy plantation owner whose lands were eventually
passed on to Thomas. Thomas married a 22 year old widow named Martha
Wayles Skelton on 01 January 1772.

Thomas Jefferson was actually born on 02 April 1743 according to the
Julian calendar in use at the time. When the English adopted the Gregorian
calendar in 1758, the date shifted forward 11 days so that today we observe
Jefferson's birth date on 13 April.

Credited with drafting the Declaration of Independence, Thomas is
recognized as one of the Founding Fathers of the United States along with
President George Washington to whom he is related through their common
ancestors of Ralph de Neville and Joan Beaufort.

During his first term as President, Jefferson commissioned Meriwether
Lewis to mount an expedition to the Pacific Coast through the recently
completed Louisiana Purchase. Although both men grew up as neighbors in
Virginia and their families were not unknown to each other, what they didn't
realize was that they were also distant cousins through their common
ancestors of Ralph de Neville and Joan Beaufort, who they also shared with
President George Washington.

Thomas Jefferson died on 04 JULY 1826, on the same day as his friend and
former political rival President John Adams. Probably unknown to
both Jefferson and Adams was that Jefferson was related to Adams's son,
President John Quincy Adams, through his wife **Abigail SMITH**.

The famous family relationships of President Thomas Jefferson are
numerous and include many notable figures from both American and
European history. Famous for his own writing, Thomas counts numerous
celebrated authors among his kin. His Royal connections go all the way back
to Charlemagne in the 8th century, and to as recent as today with family

relationships to both the bride and the groom of the recent royal wedding between <u>Catherine "Kate" Middleton</u> and <u>Prince William</u>, now the Duke and Duchess of Cambridge.

George Washington
1st U.S. President

- <u>George Washington</u>: 11th cousins 1 time removed

John Quincy Adams
6th U.S. President

- <u>John Quincy Adams</u> (1767-1848): 12th cousins 2 times removed

Alexander Hamilton
1st U.S. Secretary of the Treasury

- <u>Alexander Hamilton</u>: 12th cousins 2 times removed

Meriwether Lewis

Meriwether Lewis
Lewis & Clark - Corps of Discovery

- <u>Meriwether Lewis</u>: 11th cousins 2 times removed

General Robert E. Lee
Army of Northern Virginia

- <u>General Robert E. Lee</u> (1807-1870): 11th cousins 2 times removed

Alfred the Great
King of the Anglo-Saxons

- <u>Alfred the Great</u> (849-_): 29th great-grandfather

Charlemagne
King of the Franks and "Father of Europe"
<u>Charlemagne</u> (742-814): 31st great-grandfather

Prince William
Duke of Cambridge

- <u>Prince William</u>: 4th cousins 8 times removed

Catherine "Kate" Middleton
Duchess of Cambridge

- <u>Kate Middleton</u>: 11th cousins 9 times removed

Ray Bradbury
Author, "The Martian Chronicles"

- Ray Douglas Bradbury: 30th cousins 1 time removed

Harriet Martineau
Author, "The Hour and the Man"
Harriet Martineau: 11th cousins 3 times removed

Truman Capote
Author, "In Cold Blood"

Harper Lee
Author, "To Kill a Mockingbird"